My backyard
community

Bobbie Kalman

🌳 Crabtree Publishing Company
www.crabtreebooks.com

Created by Bobbie Kalman

Author and Editor-in-Chief
Bobbie Kalman

Educational consultants
Elaine Hurst
Joan King
Reagan Miller

Editors
Joan King
Reagan Miller
Kathy Middleton

Proofreader
Crystal Sikkens

Design
Bobbie Kalman
Katherine Berti

Photo research
Bobbie Kalman

Production coordinator
Katherine Berti

Prepress technician
Katherine Berti

Photographs
iStockphoto: p. 21 (bottom left)
All other photographs by Shutterstock

Library and Archives Canada Cataloguing in Publication

Kalman, Bobbie, 1947-
    My backyard community / Bobbie Kalman.

(My world)
Includes index.
ISBN 978-0-7787-9448-6 (bound).--ISBN 978-0-7787-9492-9 (pbk.)

    1. Urban ecology (Biology)--Juvenile literature.
I. Title. II. Series: My world (St. Catharines, Ont.)

QH541.5.C6K34 2010   j577.5'6   C2009-906107-4

Library of Congress Cataloging-in-Publication Data

Kalman, Bobbie.
 My backyard community / Bobbie Kalman.
   p. cm. -- (My world)
 Includes index.
 ISBN 978-0-7787-9492-9 (pbk. : alk. paper) -- ISBN 978-0-7787-9448-6
(reinforced library binding : alk. paper)
 1. Backyard gardens--Juvenile literature. 2. Nature--Juvenile literature.
I. Title. II. Series.

 SB473.K35 2010
 577.5'6--dc22
                                                              20090412280

Crabtree Publishing Company

Printed in China/122009/CT20091009

www.crabtreebooks.com   1-800-387-7650

Published in Canada
Crabtree Publishing
616 Welland Ave.
St. Catharines, Ontario
L2M 5V6

Published in the United States
Crabtree Publishing
PMB 59051
350 Fifth Avenue, 59th Floor
New York, New York 10118

Published in the United Kingdom
Crabtree Publishing
Maritime House
Basin Road North, Hove
BN41 1WR

Published in Australia
Crabtree Publishing
386 Mt. Alexander Rd.
Ascot Vale (Melbourne)
VIC 3032

What is in this book?

Full of living things

A **back yard** is a place behind a home. It is a place to have fun outdoors. It is also a place full of **living things**. Living things are plants, animals, and people. What kind of living thing are you?

What is a community?

A back yard is a **community**.
A community is a place that
a group of living things shares.
To stay alive, living things
need other living things.
The living things in
back yards help
one another.

Flowers and butterflies
are living things.

What are non-living things

Back yards also have **non-living things**. Non-living things are air, sunlight, rocks, water, **soil**, and things made by people. Living things need non-living things.

sunlight

slide made by people

soil

rock

water

9

Backyard plants

My back yard has many plants.
Trees, bushes, grass, weeds,
and flowers are plants.

weeds

flowers

tree

bushes

grass

Animals that eat plants

Living things need food to stay alive.
Plants make their own food from
sunlight, air, and water.
Plants are then eaten
by many animals.
Animals that eat plants
are called **herbivores**.
Squirrels, rabbits, and
butterflies are herbivores.

squirrel

butterfly

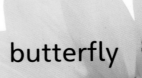

Rabbits eat grasses and flowers in back yards.
They eat vegetables from people's gardens, too.

Backyard insects

Many **insects** live in my back yard.

Insects are small animals with six legs.

Insects eat different kinds of food.

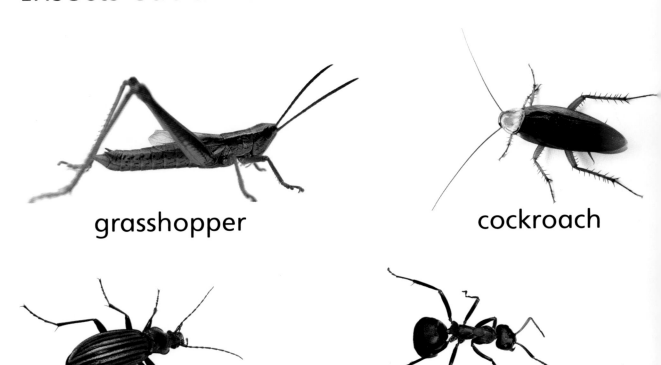

grasshopper

cockroach

beetle

ant

Some insects have wings and can fly.

dragonfly

ladybug

fly

butterfly

mosquito

bee

wasp

moth

15

Eating other animals

Some backyard animals
eat other animals.
Animals that eat other
animals are called **carnivores**.
Dragonflies and many kinds
of birds are carnivores.
Frogs are carnivores, too.

dragonfly

robin

frog

Cats are carnivores that sometimes hunt birds.

They eat everything!

Some backyard animals are **omnivores**.
Omnivores eat both plants and animals.
Raccoons, chipmunks, skunks, and
some kinds of birds are omnivores.
They eat any food they can find.

chipmunk

skunk

sparrow

This raccoon is eating bread that it found in the garbage can in my back yard.

Community helpers

Communities have helpers.

There are many helpers in my back yard.

Plants make food for bees.
Bees help new plants grow.

Bees make honey from flowers.
People eat the honey bees make.

slug

Slugs and ants
eat dead things.
They help clean
back yards.

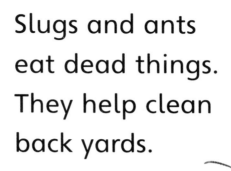

ant

Earthworms
help make
good soil.

More plants
grow in
good soil.

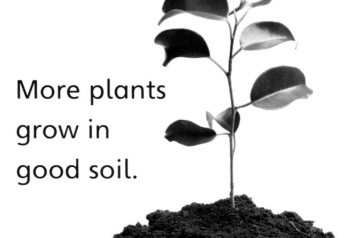

21

Be a backyard helper!

My backyard community helps me.
How can I help my backyard community?

I can help plant
a garden.
I can help plant
new trees.
I can help rake
the leaves.

I can help feed the birds in winter.

Words to know and Inde

carnivores
pages 16–17

food pages 12,
14, 18, 20

helpers pages
20–21, 22–23

herbivores
pages 12–13

insects
pages 14–15

living things
pages 4–5, 6, 7,

non-living things
pages 8–9

omnivores
pages 18–19

plants pages 4
10–11, 12, 18, 20,